Reckless LOVE

DANIEL KOLENDA

This is not a coincidence.

Someone gave you this booklet for a reason. There is a purpose at work in your life right now beyond anything you can imagine. You know it. You can feel it. It's as though the universe itself is trying to send you a message. You've been looking for a sign. This is it!

Rest assured—I'm not trying to sell you anything. This booklet is a very short read with a very powerful message that can change your life—if you will just let down your defenses for a moment.

What I am going to share with you over the next few pages is a story that has been told for thousands of years. Stories this old are more than mere stories. They have been passed down from generation to generation for a reason. The story in this booklet has stood the test of time because it contains truth that transcends culture, gender, religion, race, ethnicity, geographical location, and time. It is a truth that touches the very hearts of men and women in ways that are deeper than we may ever understand.

In fact, this story is so important, especially in Western culture, that it has been the theme of countless books, dramas, homilies and works of art—like the Rembrandt painting featured on the cover of this book. Rembrandt, by the way, is considered one of the greatest visual artists in history,[1] and that painting, known as *The Return of the Prodigal Son*, is widely considered his greatest work. Moreover, the famous art historian Kenneth Clark claimed that it is not only *Rembrandt's* greatest painting, but "the greatest picture *ever* painted" (emphasis mine).[2] The greatest painting of all time—about one of the greatest stories ever told. Certainly, this is a story every educated and cultured person should become more familiar with!

In the interest of full disclosure—as you may have already realized—this booklet is about a story from the Bible. This might immediately turn some people off, but don't worry, it has nothing to do with joining a particular church or certain denomination. It's actually not about religion at all—so relax ☺.

This booklet is about one of the most powerful and memorable stories in the Bible, commonly known as, "The Prodigal Son." Now, you may have heard the story of "The Prodigal Son" before. You might have heard it a thousand times. Maybe you grew up in the church and you know this story by heart. I want to challenge you just to keep reading for the next few minutes, because you are going to see something you have never seen before.

On the other hand, maybe you don't know the story well, but you have heard something about it. Maybe you've seen depictions like Rembrandt's famous painting and you've wondered what it's all about. Or maybe you

have no idea what I'm talking about right now and you're hearing about it for the first time. Even better! You are about to discover one of the greatest stories ever told!

The story of "The Prodigal Son" (the same one depicted in that famous Rembrandt painting) was originally told by Jesus—a man who stands out from all others like a sparkling diamond against the dark backdrop of human history. To say he is a remarkable personality is the understatement of the century.

The Most Influential Man in History

One author wrote of Jesus Christ:

He never wrote a book. He never held an office. He never had a family or owned a home. He didn't go to college. He never lived in a big city. He never traveled more than 200 miles from the place where he was born. He did none of the things that usually accompany greatness. He had no credentials but himself...

Twenty centuries have come and gone, and today he is the central figure of the human race. I am well within the mark when I say that all the armies that ever marched, all the navies that ever sailed, all the parliaments that ever sat, all the kings that ever reigned—put together—have not affected the life of man on this earth as much as that one, solitary life.[3]

The famous evangelist Billy Sunday said:

The effect of His teaching upon the world has been wonderful. Remember that He left no great colleges

to promulgate His doctrines, but committed them to a few humble fishermen, whose names are now the most illustrious in all history. Looked at from the human side alone, how great was the probability that everything He had said would be forgotten within a few years. He never wrote a sermon. He published no books. Not a thing He said was engraved upon stone or scrolled upon brass, and yet His doctrines have endured for two thousand years. They have gone to the ends of the earth and have wrought miracles wherever they have gone. They have lifted nations out of darkness and degradation and sin, and have made the wilderness to blossom as the rose...

When Jesus fed the five thousand with a few loaves and fishes and healed the poor woman who touched the hem of His garment, there wasn't a church, or a hospital, or an insane asylum, or other [charitable institution] in the world, and now they are nearly as countless as the sands upon the seashore.

When the bright cloud hid Him from the gaze of those who loved Him with a devotion that took them to martyrdom, the only record of His sayings was graven upon their hearts, but now libraries are devoted to the consideration of them. No words were ever so weighty or so weighed as those of Him who was so poor that He had nowhere to lay His head. The scholarship of the world has sat at His feet with bared head, and has been compelled to say again and again, "Never man spake as He spake."

His utterances have been translated into every known tongue and have carried healing on their wings wherever they have gone. No other book has ever had a tithe of the circulation of that which contains His words, and not only that, but His thoughts and the story of His life are so interwoven in all literature that if a man should never read a line in the Bible, and yet be a reader at all, he could not remain ignorant of the Christ.[4]

Surely you have studied many great personalities in school. Surely you have read some great books by some famous authors. But how deep is your knowledge of the words, the stories, and the teachings of Jesus Christ—the most influential man who ever lived—the man whose words literally shaped western civilization and changed the world?

We find "the prodigal son" in the fifteenth chapter of the book of Luke. Jesus said:

There was a man who had two sons. The younger one said to his father, "Father, give me my share of the estate." So he divided his property between them. Not long after that, the younger son got together all he had, set off for a distant country and there squandered his wealth in wild living.

Luke 15:11-13

The younger brother in this story did something highly unusual. He basically said, "Father, I know you're not dead yet, but I can't wait any longer. I want my inheritance now." The father had no obligation to comply with this unreasonable demand, but surprisingly, he did as his son requested. He divided up his wealth and gave the rightful portion to his younger son.

A couple days later, the son took all his money and left town. He went to the big city. Although the Bible doesn't go into great detail about what he did there, it does say that he "squandered his wealth in wild living." That means he was living recklessly. He was living for the moment. Living for the day.

It reminds me of a quote from the *Fast and Furious* movie where the lead character, a street racer, says, "I live my life a quarter mile at a time. Nothing else matters...for those ten seconds or less, I'm free."[5] It's a reckless attitude that puts pleasure and instant gratification above everything else. Nothing matters except the fleeting thrill of a few seconds of ecstasy.

His family didn't matter. His health didn't matter. His job, his reputation, the example he was to others, the impact he would make on the world and people around him, none of it mattered—he just wanted that high. He wanted that thrill. That's what he was living for. This is an attitude that's glorified in the movies and the way many people live their lives, but what a terrible way to think and live! It is incredibly selfish and irresponsible. It is short-sighted, immature, and destructive, and it leads exactly where it led the prodigal son.

> *After he had spent everything, there was a severe famine in that whole country, and he began to be in need. So he went and hired himself out to a citizen of that country, who sent him to his fields to feed pigs.*

Living Recklessly

"I live my life a quarter mile at a time. Nothing else matters...for those ten seconds or less, I'm free."

He longed to fill his stomach with the pods that the pigs were eating, but no one gave him anything.
Luke 15:14-16

This young man ended up completely destitute. He didn't have a penny to his name. His money was gone. His friends all left him. And, to make matters even worse, there was a famine in the land! People were starving all around him, and there was nothing he could do to help them—he couldn't even help himself. This is where that sort of irresponsible lifestyle leads. It's fun while it lasts, but when the famines of life come, you become a miserable, resentful, vengeful person who is of no use to yourself or anyone else. Rather than alleviating the suffering in the world, you become part of the problem. It's a terrible place to be.

Verse 14 says that he was "in need."

You see, his selfish lifestyle left this young man empty and needy. Isn't it ironic that this young man spent everything he had trying to satisfy his selfish cravings and urges, and instead of being satisfied, he ended up being needier than he was before? He caused the very thing he was trying to avoid. His cure became his disease. After spending every penny, he was hungrier than ever before—and hunger is a powerful motivator. So, he had to find more and more ways to satisfy himself. His low point came when he was forced to take a terrible job—feeding pigs and living with the pigs in the pigpen.

Now, I know this sounds unappealing to everyone. No one likes the idea of living with pigs. But you have to understand that Jesus told this story to a Jewish audience. The boy in this story was a Jewish boy, and when you realize that, it takes on new significance. For a religious Jewish boy, living with the pigs was a whole lot more than just gross…it was the ultimate picture of uncleanness and filth. Jews, of course, are not allowed to eat pork—but more than that—they avoid all association with pigs. To touch a pig carcass would make a Jew ceremonially unclean, so the fact that the boy was living with the pigs was a vivid picture of how far he had fallen. He was in a very dark place—physically, financially, relationally, and spiritually.

"I Can't Get No Satisfaction"

Not only was he living with the pigs, Verse 16 says that he longed to fill his belly with the pig's food. People who feed pigs and live with pigs soon start acting like pigs themselves. This young man's hunger had driven him to a place of desperation. He was willing to eat even the most vile, disgusting food in a frantic attempt to gratify himself. But even then, he could not satisfy his hunger.

He had started out trying to find adventure, success, love, and pleasure. But his quest led him to one dead end after another. Finally, after he had squandered everything that he had, he hit rock bottom and still was not satisfied!

It reminds me of that Rolling Stones song, "I Can't Get No Satisfaction." My friend, I meet so many people who are in that pigpen, stuffing their bellies with the most vile things in an attempt to satisfy the deep longing in their hearts. But, no matter how hard they try, they are still lonely and desperate and dissatisfied. They are hungry for something no one has been able to give them.

Some people have gone from relationship to relationship looking for satisfaction, and they keep finding themselves in abusive situations. They keep getting hurt and taken advantage of, and yet, their deep hunger for love and acceptance drives them back to the pigpen.

Many people indulge in pornography and other forms of sexual decadence in an attempt to meet some deep need. They soon find that what they are into isn't dark enough anymore. They don't get turned on by *Playboy* anymore. Now they need something more twisted, more perverted, more vile. Soon they find themselves in the darkest places, in the pit of hell itself—and yet they aren't satisfied.

Rock Bottom

The prodigal son's journey was a downward spiral that seemed impossible to get out of, until one day he woke up and thought, "How did this happen? How did I get here? Is there any help for me?"

It is in this place—when people hit rock bottom—that they often look for a way out. Some people turn to drugs or alcohol to drown out their guilt and pain. Yet, these temporary solutions don't really solve any problems, but, in fact, create new ones. Some people become murderous and hateful. They feel they have nothing to lose. They stop caring about anything and anyone—including themselves. Still, other people turn

to suicide at this point, because they are convinced there is no way to make it out of this pigpen alive.

A Moment of Clarity

So, what should you do when you find yourself in this dark place? Well, the story of the prodigal son gives us the answer:

When he came to his senses, he said, "How many of my father's hired servants have food to spare, and here I am starving to death! I will set out and go back to my father and say to him: Father, I have sinned against heaven and against you. I am no longer worthy to be called your son; make me like one of your hired servants." So he got up and went to his father...

Luke 15:17-20a

It says that, "He came to his senses." This is the moment every person needs to have. A moment of clarity. A moment of sobriety. A moment where you think, "Wait a minute. What am I doing here? What have I become? Who am I? Why am I living this way? There must be something better and something more than this in life!"

When I was about twelve-years old, my cousin started smoking. I thought it was pretty cool to stand there like James Dean in *Rebel Without a Cause* with his collar turned up, leaning against the wall with a cigarette in his hand. I wanted to be like that. So, I asked my cousin

The Moment of Clarity

if I could have a cigarette, and to my surprise, he gave me a whole pack! I never moved up in the world so fast in my life. I went from being a nobody to a cool cat, just like that. But there was a problem. If my dad caught me with cigarettes, he would kill me. And that would be kind compared to what my mother would do.

So, I took my pack of cigarettes and I went out into the woods. I sat on the ground behind a big bush and lit up one of my cigarettes. Of course, I started hacking and coughing. It was pretty miserable actually, but I thought, "Well, this is what it takes to be cool and it's worth it." I really didn't know what I was doing because the cigarette lasted a lot longer than it should have. I was determined to see it through like a man. I was determined to smoke the whole thing. But, suddenly, I had this moment of clarity. I thought to myself, "Wait a minute. I am smoking this cigarette—not because I like it—I'm smoking the cigarette to be cool. But, when I'm hiding in the woods, no one can see me. And, if no one can see me, no one can think I'm cool. If no one thinks I'm cool, what is the point? I'm going through all this for nothing." I put that cigarette out, threw the pack away, and have never smoked another cigarette since.

This story is not about smoking; this is about that moment of clarity. Some of you need to come to your senses! Maybe you grew up in the church or used to follow Jesus. You need to realize that whatever naive notions caused you to walk away from God and started you chasing after the things of this world, they didn't deliver. You didn't find the peace, joy, satisfaction, and fulfillment you were looking for. You're not even that cool. What are you doing? It's time to go home!

Maybe you've never heard these things I'm telling you before. Maybe you didn't know there was a solution to the living hell you are in. Maybe you didn't know that God has a remedy for the sin, sickness, addiction, and darkness that are trying to drown you. That's why someone put this booklet in your hands! This is your wakeup call! It's time to come home!

And that's exactly what the prodigal son did. He decided he would humble himself and go back to his father. He would offer to become one of his father's hired servants (because even they lived better than he was living).

Going Home

This is my favorite part of the story. As that young man dragged himself home, one heavy footstep at a time, he was dreading the moment when he would come face-to-face with his father. He was so worried about how his father would react to his reckless, immature life. He wasn't sure how he would explain himself when his father asked what he had done with all the money he'd been given.

Meanwhile, the father sat on the front porch with his eyes strained in the direction where his son had gone. Every day, he sat there looking, wishing, waiting, hoping that one day his son would return.

Finally, he saw the silhouette of his son appear on the horizon, and that old man could not contain himself. He got up and ran to welcome back his son!

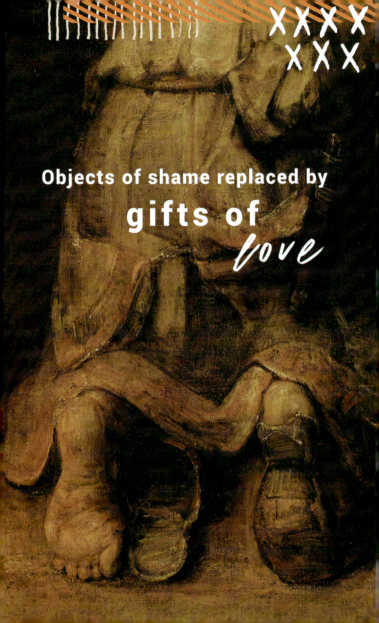

> *But while he was still a long way off, his father saw him and was filled with compassion for him; he ran to his son, threw his arms around him and kissed him.*
>
> *Luke 15:20b*

This is the scene depicted in that Rembrandt painting. The father is bending down with open hands to receive the son, who kneels before him and leans into his father's embrace. What a beautiful picture of reconciliation, of acceptance, of forgiveness, of grace and mercy! The father is not angry. He is not judgmental. He is not bitter and vengeful. He is a good father—full of compassion for the children he loves.

All the things the prodigal son had worried about so much were just a mirage. The father didn't rebuke him, punish him, or send him to live with the servants. Every day that young man had been living in the pigpen, the father was sitting on the front porch waiting for him to come home!

But, that wasn't all. The father didn't just reluctantly take him back. He hugged him, he kissed him, and he showered him with gifts like Christmas morning. He even killed the fatted calf and threw a party.

Rembrandt's painting depicts the son's tattered robe and old shoes, so worn that one has fallen off and the other one is barely hanging on. These objects of shame will be replaced with gifts of love: a new robe, new shoes, a ring for his finger, and a welcome home feast!

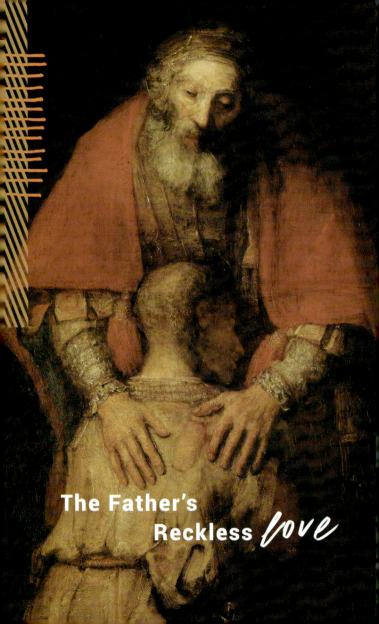

The son said to him, "Father, I have sinned against heaven and against you. I am no longer worthy to be called your son." But the father said to his servants, "Quick! Bring the best robe and put it on him. Put a ring on his finger and sandals on his feet. Bring the fattened calf and kill it. Let's have a feast and celebrate. For this son of mine was dead and is alive again; he was lost and is found." So they began to celebrate.

Luke 15:21-24

The Prodigal Father

Here is where I saw something I had never seen before. Normally, the emphasis of this story is on the son. It may be known popularly as the story of "The Prodigal Son" (as I've already referenced many times) and yet, I don't think that Jesus intended for the emphasis to be on the son at all. All along, I think it was supposed to be about the father. Notice that when Jesus started the story (in Verse 2) he didn't start by saying, "There once was a son…" Instead, Jesus begins the story like this, "A certain *man* had two sons…" (emphasis mine).

Rembrandt also managed to capture this emphasis on the father beautifully. Notice that the focus of the painting is the father. In fact, we only see the son from behind. It was the man—the father—who is the protagonist. The story is not about the son—it is about the father!

But there's more. You see, the word *prodigal* means, "wasteful, reckless, extravagant; giving or yielding profusely; lavish or abundant."[6] We say the story is about the prodigal son because we are focused on the way the son recklessly wasted his money. But, I think Jesus intended to draw our attention to the father, who freely, extravagantly, and yes, even recklessly, poured out his love and grace on his very undeserving son! I guess you could say this is the story of "The Prodigal Father."[7] Said another way, it's a story about the father's "Reckless Love."

Maybe when you think of your life, you think of all the ways that you have been wasteful and unwise. You see all your faults and failures and shortcomings. I want you to understand something. This is not about you. It's not about how far you've drifted and how much you've strayed. It's about a loving Father who loves you so much He gave everything for you. It's about a reckless love that would do anything to reach you! It's not about your reckless life—it's about God's reckless love!

One of my favorite scriptures is Romans 8:32, "He that spared not his own Son, but delivered him up for us all, how shall he not with him also freely give us all things?" God gave His Son, knowing that many people would spit in His face, reject Him, and even mock His gift of love. Yet, God freely, lavishly, and selflessly gave the best He had for you. That is reckless love. If God would give His own Son for you, you can be sure that He is willing to give you anything and everything else that you need.

This verse shows that the cross is the ultimate evidence of God's reckless love. At the cross, Jesus accepted the worst that humankind had to offer—injustice, hatred, prejudice, pride, violence, betrayal, and murder. Without a fight, He took the sins of the world upon Himself. And in return, He gave the best that God has to offer—forgiveness, humility, gentleness, generosity, faithfulness, truthfulness, salvation, and love. But, the cross is more than a symbol; it is the very means whereby God is able to extend mercy and justice while remaining completely righteous. You see, if God had simply ignored our sin, that would have been unjust. But, if we all received the justice we deserve, we would all be damned. Instead, Jesus took our punishment upon Himself (justice) and offers us forgiveness and peace with God on His account (mercy).

The Logo of Hope

As my mentor Reinhard Bonnke wrote regarding the cross of Christ:

Jesus, the carpenter of Nazareth, turned the wood of the cross into the door to life. That is the deep heart of the good news — the cross has the power to transform us. Minus is turned to plus, negative to positive. On the cross, darkness changes to light, death to life, hate to love, chains to freedom, fear to faith, despair to joy, brokenness to wholeness, hell to heaven...

The Logo of Triumph

Jesus is still alive! He is here today to reverse every curse and to cancel Satan's evil work. Sinners are forgiven. The sick are made well. Broken relationships are restored. Against the power of Jesus on the cross, the forces of evil are finally defeated.

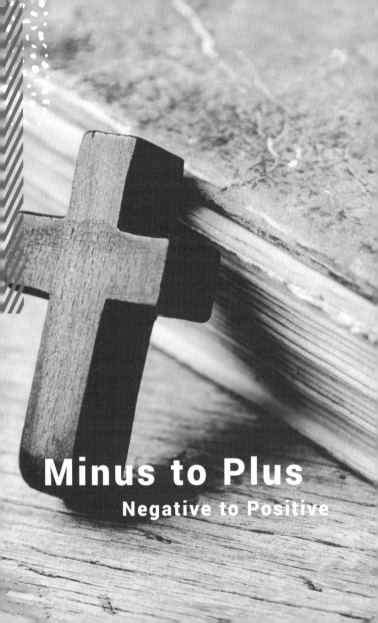

The Logo of Help

This is why the cross is the symbol or logo of the Christian faith. It belongs to Jesus alone. No founder or leader of another religion would dare to use this logo because it stands for something that they themselves have never done! None of them have been crucified for the sins of the world. None of them have been raised from the dead. None of them can give us the help we so desperately need.

Only Jesus is able to save us. As He said, "I am the way, the truth, and the life! ... Without me, no one can go to the Father."[8]

Jesus Is Calling You Out of the Darkness

In Rembrandt's painting, the father and son are illuminated against the dark backdrop of an infinite void. That is what the prodigal son came out of. He was in a world of darkness, a world devoid of light and warmth. This is a world that so many people find themselves in right now. Some people have grown so accustomed to the darkness that they enjoy it. Like zombies afraid to step into the light, the world is full of nightwalkers who have become comfortable in the darkness.

John 3:19 says, "This is the verdict: Light has come into the world, but people loved darkness instead of light because their deeds were evil."

But in this story of the prodigal son, Jesus is calling us out of the darkness into the light and the warmth of God's embrace. You don't have to live a meaningless life

anymore. You don't have to wander in exile anymore. You can come home to a fire and a feast—to love and acceptance. You are invited into a family where you belong and where you are loved. That is the Gospel.

I Am the Prodigal Son

There is one more interesting detail in Rembrandt's most famous painting. It's a detail most are not aware of. The prodigal son in the painting is a self-portrait of Rembrandt. He inserted himself into the story. He's saying, "I am the prodigal son."

This is the real point of "The Prodigal Son." Jesus wasn't just telling a parable about some random Jewish boy—He was telling the story of us. It's my story. It's your story. It's an invitation to insert yourself into the greatest drama of all time. Wherever you find yourself today—if you are in a faraway land, if you are trying to fill your soul with things that don't satisfy, if you are living with the pigs or longing for home—today is your day. I pray you would have that moment of clarity as the prodigal son had in the pigsty—that you would come to yourself and realize you don't have to live this way anymore.

No matter where you are right now, no matter how far you've wandered or how lost you feel, you can come home today! The Bible says there are two things you need to do—repent and believe the Gospel (the good news).

Repent and believe the good news!

Mark 1:15

Repent

To repent means to turn around. If you are walking in the wrong direction, you need to stop and turn around and start moving in the right direction. The prodigal son had to change his direction—to stop walking away from his father and start walking toward home.

But, even more importantly, he had to change the way he was thinking. He thought of his father as judgmental and harsh. He feared returning to him until he realized that if he went home, even the worst-case-scenario was better than his current condition. This is also what repentance means—not just a change of direction, but a change in the way you think. The Bible gives us a new way of thinking about God and about ourselves—and when we embrace that new way of thinking, that is repentance.

So, what is this new way of thinking? First, we need to change our minds about ourselves—we need to see ourselves the way God sees us. Most people think that they are basically good people. They surely aren't as bad as some others they know. They don't think they are lost, and they don't think they need any help. But the Bible says that the heart of man is "deceitful above all things, and desperately sick; who can understand it?" (Jeremiah 17:9 ESV). It says that we have all gone astray like lost sheep (Isaiah 53:6), that none of us are righteous and none of us deserve God's mercy (Romans 3:10), and that we are all sinners in need of a Savior. The prodigal son said to his father, "*Father, I have sinned against heaven and against you.*" He realized that he wasn't worthy of forgiveness, but he threw himself upon his father's mercy. When we see ourselves as sinners needing God's undeserved grace and mercy, we are positioned for forgiveness. James 4:6 says that "God opposes the proud but gives grace to the humble."

Second, we need to change our mind about God. He is not a fairy tale. He is not an old bearded man in the sky. He is not an angry tyrant looking to club you over the head for your mistakes. He is that loving father in the story who longs for you to come home. He created you. He sent His Son to die for you. You belong to Him, and He welcomes you home with open arms!

Believe

To believe is not simply to give mental assent to an idea. In the biblical context, it means to *fully trust*. A great illustration of this comes from John G. Payton, who was a missionary to the New Hebrides. He was translating the Bible into the local language and was looking for the right word to translate the word *believe* from English into the native tongue. He struggled for a while because he knew that the word had to indicate more than accepting an idea as true. It had to indicate total trust. One day, after he had returned from a long hunt, he collapsed, exhausted, into a chair. When one of the natives saw this, he said, "It's good to stretch yourself out and rest when you are tired." Suddenly, Payton had an epiphany. He took those words "stretch out and rest" and used them to translate the word *believe* in the native language.[9] Indeed, this is what the word *believe* means for us as well. God invites us to "stretch out and rest" on the work that Jesus did for us on the cross.

When the prodigal son returned home, he was destitute. He didn't have a penny to his name. The very clothes on his back were falling apart. He had nothing to offer his father except himself. It is only in this condition that we can come to God. He only receives those who realize they have nothing to offer but themselves. Those who think they are worthy are disqualified. This is because we cannot earn salvation, and we can never be good enough to deserve salvation. We can only receive it as a free gift.

> *For it is by grace you have been saved, through faith—and this is not from yourselves, it is the gift of God—not by works, so that no one can boast.*
> *Ephesians 2:8-9*

> *If you will respond in obedience to God's Word, you have His promise, "Everyone who calls on the name of the Lord will be saved."*
> *Romans 10:13*

If that's your desire, I would like to invite you to pray—in your own words, or by using the prayer below:

Father God, I come to you a sinner, needing salvation.

I cannot save myself, but I cast myself upon your mercy.

Take my sin, my shame, my addictions, and my darkness. Give me your righteousness, your freedom, your light, and your love.

I confess with my mouth what I believe in my heart—that Jesus is Lord and that God raised Him from the dead. I put my faith and my trust in Jesus Christ alone.

I receive your free gift of salvation through Jesus Christ. Fill me now with your Holy Spirit and make me a child of God.

As of this day, I belong to Jesus and Jesus belongs to me. I believe it, I receive it, and I confess it—in the name of Jesus, Amen!

If you have turned to God with repentance and faith, you are now a part of "the family of God"—the largest family in the world. Hundreds of millions of us have made the same decision to follow Jesus. The Bible says: "Therefore if any man be in Christ, he is a new creature: old things are passed away; behold, all things are become new" (2 Corinthians 5:17). You can be sure that God has heard your prayer. This is the first day of the rest of your life. The best is yet to come!

May I suggest one thing more for you?

If you have received Jesus as your Savior today, or if you would like more information, please go to **RECKLESSLOVE.US** and electronically fill in the form on the secure website. After you have done this and we receive your details, we will send you another booklet as a free gift. It explains your relationship with Christ and will give you some practical steps to help you grow even closer to Him.